PRAISES FOR
Poetic Convictions

Poetic Convictions is a masterpiece of writing! Through soulful verse, Jill delivers messages that resonate and gently encourage the reader to look inward, nudging growth and strength. Her convictions become the reader's convictions, but they don't dictate; rather, they invite the reader to consider his or her own place in the Universe. Themes of hope, empowerment, finding life's passion and faith, love's trials, and perseverance left me, an avid reader of poetry, feeling refreshed and renewed. In a world that increasingly uses words to disparage, Jill finds ways to shine beautiful lights into dark spaces.

— Joann R. Desy, teacher

Thoughtful. Timely. Inspiring. A must read for anyone who believes in the beauty of the range of emotions.

— JoAnn Jenkins, Counselor

As an "Endo Warrior", this book has inspired me to shift my mindset and see the silver lining.

— Janet Morano, Wife, Mom of 3

Poetic Convictions

A COLLECTION OF
POEMS, PROSE & PURPOSE

from the pen of
J. PETROWSKY

CONTENTS

Prologue: ENDometriosis 11

Convictions Of Love 13

Convictions Of Pain 37

Convictions Of Strength 58

Convictions Of Realization 80

Convictions Of Faith 104

Epilogue 127

About the Author 128

Connect with J. Petrowsky 129

Acknowledgements

A monumental thank you to my parents. You are the epitome of what support is. Without your constant love and strength this book would never have come to fruition. I love you with all of me.

To my family who stands beside me in all my endeavors, thank you for always cheering me on.

To the most amazing group of friends anyone can have, your unwavering encouragement has meant more than you will ever realize. Thank you for being there through tears and smiles.

Anthony, your support has been a pillar on this journey. Thank you.

To Kelly Myers from Simply K Studios, thank you for seeing my vision on all our photographic journeys together. Your work is untouchable.

To all my endo sisters and those that love you, you are nothing short of amazing and brave beings. Thank you for fighting and speaking openly even when it hurts.

To every person who has made me cry tears of joy or pain, who is still in my life or not a big cheer and thank you goes to you. Without all of the ups and downs and the journey of emotions I have lived thus far this book would not be possible.

Intro

This book is dedicated to the endo warriors and those that love them who are standing up and using their voices to create the change we need and to the ones that are suffering in silence. I hear you. I am with you.

Be a student to
the lessons that your
lowest of lows
&
highest of highs
will teach you
on your journey.

J.Petrowsky

PROLOGUE:
ENDometriosis

Pain affects everyone you know, even when you don't know.

Physical pain may not always be noticeable to those not enduring its wrath. Physical pain can ravage our bodies and yet we put masks on our faces with smiles drawn upon them.

Disease in seemingly able bodies is not understandable to those who can't see proof of ailment on the outside.

Physical pain creates emotional torture, social evading, financial hardship, relationship heartbreak and spiritual question.

Nights curled up in a fetal position on the floor, white knuckled and praying for reprieve go unmentioned.

I stayed silent while I bled into a pale silhouette. Fearing I might create discomfort for those that would cringe over my reality, a reality of insurmountable battles of womb and internal torment.

But pain can create something bigger than itself and that is the fight to **END** it.

END unanswered inquisitions. **END** unnecessary surgery. **END** uneducated experts. **END** aloneness. **END** unawareness.

I am saying it loud. Putting pen to paper and writing my way through it, to help in the fight against **END**ometriosis for the almost 200 million women plagued by its invasion.

CONVICTIONS OF LOVE

Love has meant so many different things to me over the years as I am sure it has to you.

I experienced heart break early on in life and it taught me that with love comes hurt. It's inevitable.

When we open ourselves up to the most amazing love, whether it be a relationship with a significant other, family member, friend or whatever that looks like to you. We expose ourselves to the hurt that follows when they are no longer around. Whether that is a relationship ending or someone we care about passing away, etc.

Often we get wrapped up in this "fairy tale" type of love and technology has made this idea of love seem even more attainable than ever. In a story or a picture one can be envious of what they think might be the "perfect love" or "perfect relationship" while never knowing the reality behind a post or picture.

Love isn't always so cut and dry and solid like we want it to be. It ebbs and flows. It seems to come and go. Love doesn't look and feel the same to everyone. Nobody has the same love story and everyone's journey is different.

Sometimes we want love to be somewhere it just cannot be found and other times we tend to shy away from the love that is given to us for whatever reason.

Once in a while we can be truly blessed with a love that outshines what we ever imagined love could ever feel like. This is rare and magnificent. Of course, this once in a lifetime love still comes with hardship, such is life, but nonetheless the love carries on.

Love looks and feels different as we go throughout life, but one thing that is certain in all of its uncertainty is that we are better for it even when it hurts.

They Roam

She was small town charm, he was city slicker

Country comfort meets lights camera action

His mind was defeated, her heart was depleted

A story unraveled in poetic motion

Wandering empty streets tagged in color

Hand in hand they roam, dreaming of a place called home

One Look

With just one look you leveled me

Barely able to speak and struggling to see

How is it that you have such abundant power

Causing even my inner lioness to cower

Love... That is why

The reason I laugh, the echo in my cry

Love...that is the reason

Because of this I change with every season

Senseless & inconvenient, beautiful and wild

My classiness sheds and I become a young child

But now that I have felt it, how do I ever go without

I'm too far gone, too enmeshed in your soul...of this there is no doubt

The One

Today my love for you means more than our yesterdays

We are far from a magical fairytale

I didn't "know" like everyone said I would that you were "the one"

I was quite certain our ending was inevitable and our time fleeting

Our minds were filled with more questions than answers

Two stories twisted together leaving both desperate for an amicable finish

Today I understand that not all experiences of falling in love are filled with butterflies and shooting stars

That you don't always "know" and that is OK

Falling in love is sometimes as literal as the term, landing on a platform of confusion and not a calming cushion of roses

We fell and got battered and bruised along the way

We chose to stand back up together while acknowledging the damage

We chose each other for this wild and unpredictable journey

Today, seeing all we have gone through and how we persevered it all makes sense

This was our story; the absolutely imperfect, beautiful, frustrating, amazing sometimes unidentifiable thing called LOVE

Today I "KNOW" you are "THE ONE"

Fable

A story of love
on a bedside table
Invoked real hopes
within pages of a fable

Home

The sight of you makes my heart

feel as if it will beat out of my chest

Without you days turn into nights

void of solace or rest

In the depths of your soul

lies the place I call home

From its warmth and security

I will never roam

Lush

Drunk on

thoughts of you

Got me feeling

like a lush

Real Love

I had to make peace

with my past

So real love

could have a

chance to last

My Find

I

LOST my way

&

FOUND my love

Never

The
PROFUNDITY
of love
is never
SIMPLE

I Say

You say...

I gave love too much power

I say...

You never felt the power of love

City Summer

We drank bourbon

under city lights

Trading dreams

on summer nights

You

You breathed life into my concave chest

Expanding my cold heart with the heat of hope

Your hands bloodied from my broken pieces

You never wavered when I shot you with words quick and painful

You sat patiently at the window to my soul

A survivor of the same pain, who refused to try and stitch me together

But instead embraced the scarred beauty who was rejecting him

Forcing me to welcome the woman I became and not the wounded girl I used to be

Because once your heart is broken, only then will you learn the depths of love

Ocean Blues

I miss you most

on smoother days

How you reveled in

the simple ways

My heart would swim

in your ocean blues

Never mine but

forever my muse

Wordplay

Throw the fancy

presents away

&

Gift me with

your wordplay

Blind

My mind is full of chapters
waiting to be read
The answers are all there
circling in my head
But when it comes to you
the heart trumps the mind
The answers aren't sought
to the chapters I am blind

Novel

My

heart

is

bleeding

novels

Falling

I pray you

have the strength

to catch me

When I fall

for you

Depths

I am lost

in the depths

of your soul

With no desire

to ever

be found

Story

The scene waiting to unfold

A story yearning to be told

Rawness and truth always transcend

Mind feverish from words on fire

A madness burning with desire

Chaos and characters wait to be penned

The Rest Will Come

Nobody completes us

We don't need to be completed

We are always growing

Before you get into a relationship

Learn and Love the uniqueness of you

The rest will follow

Head To Toe

From head to toe I knew it was you

I knew when you confronted the fear within me

Balanced me when I began to falter

I knew because of the magic I felt

When you looked at every flaw with ease

Every pain with love

From head to toe I knew it was you

CONVICTIONS OF PAIN

Pain, we have all felt it in some way. Pain manifests in all kinds of ways. Physical pain can bring on pain in all different forms. A body in agony on a regular basis faces the emotional pain of dealing with limitations of what you can and cannot do and the relationships that are challenged because of it. In reverse, emotional pain and depression can often be so debilitating we start to feel pain physically throughout our bodies. Our minds and bodies are so intricately connected it is almost hard to feel one type of pain without the other.

Relationships of all kinds, career challenges, loss of a loved one, depression battles and all of the people or thoughts that we once embraced with love can be some of the toughest mountains we will have to climb to get to the other side. If we didn't love as hard as we do, we wouldn't hurt as deeply as we do. Sometimes the way a relationship ends can throw us for more of a loop than ever anticipated. Betrayal and lies coming from someone we once trusted can feel as if we were completely knocked down. And if you yourself did something disrespectful to a loved one it can be especially painful to deal with while riddled with guilt.

Sometimes we just want to get rid of the memories we had as if that would help erase the pain we feel. It won't. But we never stop searching for a way to numb it even if it is only temporary. This journey through pain can be brutal. But there is a lesson in all of it and if you can find a reprieve from the physical element of it and get to the other side of the emotional presence of it, there is more life than you ever imagined possible to live.

Whiskey Truth

We told whiskey truths

under a smoke

filled sky

One last time

before we had to

say good bye

Between The Lines

Words eloquently laced together

with an everlasting message

AND STILL....

You choose to read between the lines

Kinks

Kinks in communication
break bonds made of stone
Sensitivities shunned by aggravation
leave hearts to beat alone

Untruth

I believe in good

I believe in truth

But I am still broken

By the evil of

untruth

Uncertainty

I get stuck in my thoughts and the torture of you

It can last seconds or hours but nothing ever new

It's gray and rocky and loud and bright

I have to make it out, so I fight

I don't think I know how to be free

Do I trust you,

Do I even trust me

Bourbon Blindness

The words just keep rolling off my paper tongue

I light fire to pages of thoughts and frame loveless quotations

I stood firm in the wake of you

Sipping blindness from bourbon

Maryjane inhalations and distracted flirtations

Tripped over patrons and martyrs with broken desires

Bitter redemption welcomes comical salvation

Powerful Pain

Some pain

leaves you

blind

Some pain

forces your

eyes open

Corner Of My Mind

Somewhere in a little

corner of my mind

you took residence

I try to pretend

you've moved

but I always

feel your presence

Two Souls One Bottle

We were

two broken hearts

with one

bottle of whiskey

Just two

unsettled souls

Seeking one refuge

Sharing two

rueful stories

While toasting to

one ending

Stitches

You stitched yourself together

with convenient lies

&

I pulled the thread exposing the

Inconvenient truth

The Sea

There is a story of lost love in every tear
Creating a sea filled with hearts and memories
Some are fleeting and easy to move on from
Others are so vivid they chain you to a moment
I had dropped enough stories into the deep
Breathed the air of salt and sadness
Heard the waves cry as they crashed
I grew terrified of this sea full of stories
Careful never to linger too long by its edge
Yet I was drawn here somehow
Knowing one day I would wade in its waters
Facing my pain and cleansing my wounds

Behind The Walls

Behind the walls

of a

house furnished with loneliness

lies a weeping soul

Backwards

Pain

brought us

together

Love

ended up

sabotaging us

Preferably

I would rather

you break me

with the truth

than love me

with a lie

When The Storm Came

The day I lost you

was the day the storm came to our doorstep and

immersed us

Hammering our home and breaking down

our walls

Damaging winds and torrential rains

pulled off any signs

of security

When the sun began

to shine again

I was illuminated in the

bareness of

solitude

Homeless

My feet

walked away

but my heart

stayed behind

My body

now an empty shell

and my love

hath no home

Devastations Eye

I am in the eye of the storm

The pain is almost unbearable

I am going to stay in its wrath for the duration

Don't guide me out of its volatility

Don't soothe me with encouragement

I refuse to be picked up off the floor in this moment

I want to lay here and feel every bit of this agony

I want to dwell in this despair I feel

Because when I finally get up

When I stand on my own two feet

I will never allow myself to be hit like this again

Ever

Beds Of Bones

Violent fists shattering a cheekbone

Innocent eyes watch silent

Swallowing scars manifesting adhesions embedded in a reaction

that now crushes cartilage

Light feet, dark hands born from strength of powerful ancestors

Belittled for difference

Hardened by bullied mouths

Now condemn individuality

Laying on beds of bones and looking through ash filled lids we cry

Cry for a change out of reach

As the most gospel of man can never walk in pure honor

I'm Sorry

Maybe love takes a practice I don't have patience for

My broken pieces cut deeper into wounds craving to heal

Karma collected hearts I broke and shot a bullseye in my core

My misery had to stop the constant spinning of the wheel

I am sorry for hurting you

I made my hurt too big to see your pain

I was a victim and in turn made one out of you

Please forgive me for my cold attempts so vain

I hope your peace will be enough to raise my heart anew

CONVICTIONS OF STRENGTH

On the other side of that pain, there lies strength.

Learning to be strong can be one of the hardest challenges for all of us. There are times I want to just tune everything out curl up into a ball and do nothing. But I can't. I just won't. The world is going to keep on turning regardless of whether we stay stagnant or not.

How we deal with adversity and the challenges in our lives is what will make or break us. We have to rise up to the occasion even if we don't want to. If we don't pull from our own inner strength we won't move forward. We have to be strong for ourselves. For what we believe in and for what and who we love. Nobody can take from you what you do not give them.

Going through the process of pain and learning how to stand on two feet again creates a courage and strength inside you that can change the entire course of your life. We are often so much stronger than we realize. Once you go through some of life's challenges there is a fire that is ignited inside of you. Knowing that powerful and beautiful blaze exists, will allow you to move the mountains you once had to climb.

Our Path

At times

we must walk

our path alone

It is here we will

find strength

Here we learn about self

&

let our power ignite

Then we can see in a way

we never have before

And find our way home on a path

blazed in light

About Time

I cut fear off at the neck and anguish from my tongue

Let my excuses burn alongside a box full of pain

I got real with myself as I stared at my crazed reflection

I showed up for myself and let the savaging negativity go

Your Journey

When YOU know within yourself that amazing things are coming

THEY create negative buzz and get the haters humming

Let THEM battle with bitterness and grapple with greed

While YOU embrace YOUR journey and find strength to succeed

Bold

She is glitter and gold

&

All things BOLD

Embrace & Welcome

Embrace your *WILD*

Find

Your

CALM

Welcome *BALANCE*

I Chose

I waited • I was jaded • Because of you

I cried • You lied • It's all true

Every song • All the wrong • Reminded me

Of time lost • Years cost • I wasn't free

From the start • Punished my heart • Then one day

Open eyes • I cut ties • I walked away

I earned • I learned • Prayed from deep

Built new • I grew • Peace filled sleep

Now anointed • Finger pointed • At my own face

I chose • Those woes • Closed case

Worth now known • In my zone • Feet are grounded

Second chance • Strong stance • Faith has sounded

Veracious

Be
VERACIOUS
in a world
full of
TRICKERY

Take Back

Don't keep giving weakness

your heart to

devour

Find strength within yourself and

take back your

power

Mornings

Each Morning she dresses

Pain up with Promise

Apprehension with Ability

Steps into Security

&

Walks in Wonderment

Let Them

You know your worth

SO

Let the haters hate

Let the cheaters mate

&

KEEP ROCKING

Breathe

If you feel your heart breaking

Then your lungs are still breathing

Inhale the blessing

Exhale the pain

Beauty And The Beast

Early grind with the rest of the hustle hard

Emotionally invested with armor on guard

Healing from struggles and wounds full of salt

Running the road traveled by the least

Inside this beauty rumbles a beast

Seeking depths in souls and higher exalt

Action

Don't just

SPEAK it

LIVE it

Answer

When your passion

calls

Don't let it go

unanswered

Go

Even when

your morale

is on low

Keep your head

in the game

AND GO!

Allowance

Nobody can control you without you allowing them to

You are responsible for giving away your power

Nobody else

Stop pointing fingers outward when the issue is inward

You can't blame someone else for what you allow to transpire

If you don't like something, find your strength and change it

Protect the amazing being that is

YOU

Dear Darkness

You became a comfort to me
A place to sit in sadness
mingle with misery and
lay with loneliness
during my bitter blues
But darkness, I don't regret you
In fact, I needed you
If it wasn't for your presence
and your hold so heavy
I wouldn't have searched for strength
or grew tired of dreary days and
unchallenged chapters

I grew into my own guide
braved my internal battles and
found my own light
I may visit you again one day
Because life includes you at times
But now that I know the power within me
I know I won't stay with you very long
I am too focused on forward
married to movement and
in awe of my awareness
to dwell in a home with you

In That Order

ASSIMILATE

MOTIVATE

ELEVATE

Hey Beautiful

That unmentionable pain you carry

It doesn't define you

so, own it and use it

to design

you

Wild Horses

She was alluring beauty

like wild horses

Racing through terrain

Slowing down barely long enough for you to catch a glimpse

Never close enough to let you catch her

Drinking nature and bathing in freedom

Chained to none

Mysteriously captivating in a land of mundane

She was strength of heart

Brilliance of mind

Prancing through life in power

Wild and free

CONVICTIONS OF REALIZATION

This is where the magic happens, in the realizations of it all. You loved, endured, battled, lost some and won some and here you are. You know more than you did. You are much wiser for all you have been through. I know I am. I have learned so many lessons as I am sure you have too. I am stronger and much more protective over myself than I have ever been. I believe in my choices. I am not mistake free but I am much more confident in my wants and more selective with my needs. I am aware that life can change in an instant and I am ok with not always knowing how or what to do. We can never stop learning and being open to what life has to teach us.

Through the love, pain and strength building I have realized so much about myself and what I will and will not tolerate. This world is riddled with catastrophe leaving many to go on a journey of peace. It starts with self. When we learn to love who we are as individuals it is much easier to embrace the differences in everyone, we can deal with adversity better than we ever could before.

Realization of self is a powerful tool. Use it!

Misery Loves Company

Sometimes when you're happy or have a positive attitude

it pisses miserable people off

LET IT

It's OK to be down or go through drama sometimes

that's a part of life

But

DON'T BE THE COMPANY

MISERY KEEPS

Simple Complication

The

truth

is

simple

Our

perceptions

create

the

complication

Lost & Found

In the throes of chaos and monumental

LOSS

Clarity and life changing revelations are often

FOUND

Just Don't

Don't tell me

about your come

UP

If you had to knock someone

DOWN

to get there

Time

TIME

is

NEVER

CONSIDERED

as

MUCH

as it is

UNTIL

it

RUNS OUT

Not Today

In my darkest of times when I felt the world might swallow me whole,

you let the wind carry you away

The storm has passed now, my shine is bright

Like a bird you want to fly home

but no my dear...

not today

Body And Soul

Your beautiful body and muscle strength

mean nothing if your soul is weak

Put down the weights for a day

Get in tune with what your heart has to say

Empathy

Unfortunately most people don't know the difference between being sympathetic and being empathetic.

If you know a soul who understands this,

Cherish them

Learn from them

Heal with them

Some Days

Some days I am

WHISPERS

of poetry and prose

Others I am rap music

LOUD

and full of base

Life

Change is inevitable

You may loathe today what you love tomorrow

Life shifts constantly

Your never could actually be your forever

You have to be open

Allow yourself to be kicked out of your comfort zone

Let it be

Be ok with observing from the audience

And cherish the moment when you take the stage

Life has intricate twists and turns

Some days you need to hang on

Some you need to let go

Such is life

Understanding

Whether it was passed on from generation to generation, taught through experience, ingrained in our minds since we were children or has changed over time, we all have different ideologies.

No matter if we believe to our core that our words are the truth, we should never fail to realize there are amazing souls who read from a different Scripture, fight for a different purpose, breathe a different reality and learn from a different teacher.

Yes there is fear of the unknown. So seek the knowledge and reasoning behind why a home is filled with the words it lives by. Understanding is the only way to create the bridge those of us seeking peace need to build.

Mind Full

My mind

is a musician

seeking

lyrical invocation

Broken Beauty

Your

broken

pieces

are

beautiful

Almost 20

As each season passes it swallows a piece of my youth
Each layer shed shows a little more of the forbidden truth
It seems so strange, the trials of life
Yet it awakens our soul, makes us stronger through strife
The wishes made, the words unsaid, those chances missed
The ones you loved yesterday, today the one you kissed
The games you played, the situations you refused
The unknown adventure that left us amused
The safe smiles and laughter that makes you want to cry
The suffocating silence when it's time for goodbye
The feeling of anguish inside, that you pray won't last
The will of good faith within that pushes you passed

We all get here, somehow in different ways
Some fast, some hindered with delays
We all cross paths for a justified reason
What you lost last winter I could find next season
Condemn me not for we are all one
Living and breathing under one sun
Dealing with memories of that unforgettable face
Searching for answers to get us through life's race
We have to keep going no matter how hard life seems
Accept all your mistakes and live out your dreams

Negativity Has No Home Here

My ears couldn't hear the gossip you told

My eyes didn't see that shade you threw

My brain won't process that negativity

My world is bigger than senseless chatter

You want to know what does matter

My heart beats crazy love

My lungs fill up with this beautiful life

Tomorrow is never promised

My soul will always pray for you

Let the hurt you cause yourself cease

May your lips be a vessel for peace

Shed the weakness you must feel

Become the goodness you were meant to be

Freedom Of Self

On the exterior you're a rock capable of

withstanding wicked woes and heavy hardship

A shoulder for the insecure to lean upon

with a smile to encourage the tearful

But within your interior lies the truth

You are breaking from burden and the

collection of stories crying for completion

Your empathetic heart is hurting dear friend

Don't be afraid to let the river flow

Break the binding restraints of misplaced responsibilities

We need balance to breathe so

FEEL IT & FREE IT

For Peace

MUTE HATE

LOVE LOUD

Dear Little Sister

Don't follow my footsteps.

I wish for something greater for you.

Walk your own path while you learn from my missteps.

I don't want to scare you but I want to be honest with you.

This world can be very, very cold.

You will endure or see others endure things that will stay in your mind forever.

These moments will change you.

Don't let them make you bitter.

Allow them to make you even better.

Don't let hate harden who you are.

Keep a soft heart because that is what will make you brave.

Become friends with people from all over the world,
of all religions and colors.

Go to their homes and learn about their traditions.

When you start to make a difference people are going to
attempt to sit you down.

You stand up tall for who you are and what you believe.

Relish in moments of love and laughter because this is
what counts in the end.

Write down your dreams and speak them out loud.

Don't ever let anyone tell you they are not attainable.

Believe, no matter the disbelief around you.

You will meet people that may seem as if they will be
with you a lifetime.

They won't always be. People in our lives tend to come and go.

Usually, except for a select few that will walk with you forever.

Don't let the hurt you feel consume you.

Remember that they were in your life for a lesson
and removed for a reason

Remember that heartbreak is inevitable and will happen
in some way somehow.

Allow yourself to feel it, I promise even though it will seem you cannot bare
it, you will get through.

One day you will be able to look back on it and be able to reflect honestly
on the experience.

And the next time you fall in love make sure this special someone makes
your heart dance.

Reach little sister. Reach sky high.

Let the impossible become possible in all facets of your life.

Live, little sister.

Live every day openly and honestly. Soak up the wisdom and cherish what makes you smile.

Learn little sister.

Learn every day until you are no longer walking on this earth. Learning is a never-ending process.

Teach little sister.

Teach others to live and love and find beauty in the ugliness.

This life is not pain free, but it is the most important gift you will ever receive so live and love and make it count and remember always... that I love you.

CONVICTIONS OF FAITH

*T*he root of it all.. is the faith we carry. This will be different for everyone from all walks of life.

Today as we witness all of the disparities in our world our faith is at the forefront.

So many believe that no other belief system then their own is worthy and all others are condemned. Wars are being battled leaving lands full of death and demise.

Yet there are many of us that are holding onto hope. Learning to love and respect our neighbors, coming together in a search for peace. We are teaching our children to embrace all, illuminating the open minded and standing strong together.

Faith is a light in the midst of darkness and a friend in the valley of loneliness. It has the power to keep those teetering on the edge grounded and is healing warmth for so many. Faith can be the hand we hold as we go through the trials and tribulations of life. Faith can be the water we add to the soil of our relationships that enables them to grow and flourish.

No matter what book your prayers are in, celebration you toast to or home you reside in; let your faith guide you to goodness.

Have faith in the amazingness of life and create peace as you walk your journey. Let the love and faith you feel shine so bright that the world can't help but to see and feel it.

Of Minds And Mouths

Fire on tongues of restless souls
Leave an aftermath of wreckage like burning coals
Products of generations from blinding pain
Render too many thoughts ignorant and vain
Terror and fear the unfortunate commonality of our youth
Pasts of blame creating futures without truth
But what if we stopped listening with eager ears
Started learning through eyes immersed in tears
Woke up from a long conforming sleep
Purged the darkness that resonates so deep
Reached for unity so foreign in our times
Would it lessen a world so violent in crimes

Think for ourselves and begin to self-teach
Mend as many broken pieces as our strength can reach
Believe in a difference in division we could possibly make
Using one person's power to heal for another's sake
Don't sit idle by my side in a world so cold
If I will. You will. If you will. They will. Be bold.

Storm & Solace

Those choppy waters you have to endure during the storm

are the same waters you look to for solace

Navigate wisely through the rough times and embrace the calmness

that is sure to follow

Prayer Warriors

Too many souls

desolate & depressed

Unaware of prayer warriors

void of any rest

Light

In times of

Inevitable darkness

BE

THE

LIGHT

Blossom

Just as the sun

can shine after rain

A masterpiece

can blossom from pain

Words

Use the blessing of your words in love, honor and faith

Words can start the battle of a thousand wars across the land

Words can end the battle of a thousand wars across the land

Music

When music is in your soul

You can sing to sorrow

And dance with faith

Pray

When the darkness starts to settle inside of your soul

PRAY

When you're beginning to lack all of your control

PRAY

When you need the chaos to quiet and the fight to cease

PRAY

When your heart is full and your mind is at peace

PRAY

When you're joyful and happy in life

PRAY

When you experience struggle and strife

PRAY

There are hopes, dreams and thoughts we need to convey

Embrace the power and strength above and

PRAY

Everyday

Live the life you choose

Win every time you lose

Protect your amazing soul

Make faith your daily goal

If it hurts then walk away

When it feels right stay

Put a smile on your beautiful face

Make this world a better place

Rest

Unrest lies in the belly of the unanswered, hearts of the discontented

and minds of the uninvited.

Invite yourself to acceptance of what is known in the moments of today

so contentment breeds new rest

Stay Lit

In moments of hopelessness

When the cold of the darkness seems to paralyze you

Start moving even if you can't see in front of you

Your courage will spark

Allowing your path to glow with light and everlasting warmth

Prayer Volume

Let's mesh our souls

together

&

Turn up our prayers to the highest

volume

Vibes

If you feel a vibration in the presence of someone, trust it.

Vibes speak loudly without saying a word

Let the trust in the vibe

Create faith in your guide

Take Cover

Let's cover each other in light

Allow ourselves humility

Commit to our relationships

&

Be the bridge to betterment

The Key

During the biggest times of failure

The greatest moments of success

There was a constant flicker inside me

This was the key to every door

A key to self-awareness

The ultimate gift of encouragement

Walk With You

I walk with you on this journey

Through rocky roads and sandy streets

Sunny days and rainy skies

Through good times and painful decisions

Fleeing moments and forever farewells

I walk with you in faith

Through everything

Now and always

Temple Of Love

The blood of my ancestors beats through my heart

Their will to survive carries on with every breath

Generations removed from the horror they faced

Our world has new battles but the root is still the same

Peace seekers bond in a pact of interfaith

Shaking the tree of the unwilling

Let them unearth we say

The spewed disparage won't harden our eager minds

I walk with my brothers and sisters in a mosaic wave

As we enter our home in the temple of love

I Am Water

I was in a dam

Contained and comfortable

Until the day my levee broke

I flowed about forcefully

I couldn't control the current

There was chaos and fear

How do I protect others from my wrath with no barrier

How would I rebuild

Then I remembered

I am water

I am beautiful and peaceful

I am dangerous and mysterious

I am prayed for

Community will join together to reconstruct

Fear will bring love

Love will bring appreciation

Hope will swim within me

Faith is in the sky I rest under

I am water

I will survive

Epilogue

What are your convictions?

Do they make you proud and add meaning to your life?

Our lives are all different. The web of life is so intricate and ever changing.

Our journeys consist of constant learning and along the way we adopt different assurances.

Whatever you claim to be your own conviction; Make it good. Make it count. Make it honest and Make it matter to you and all who know you.

About the Author

Jill Petrowsky has been writing since she was a child. Her love of words has become her lifestyle. With all of life's twists and turns she has used her words for healing through some of life's toughest moments, communication and happiness. Jill says each emotion can evoke inspiration so she is never far from a pen and paper as each day brings something new.

Uniquely, Jill mixes poetry, prose, quotes and notes about life into her collection and in turn has helped countless people that have embarked on her journey of words feel that they are not alone and hopeful. Each piece carries a message that someone needs to hear.

Jill's first poem was published in a booklet titled "A Woman's Book" when she was a teenager.

Jill was born and raised in Connecticut.

She is an animal lover who can be found advocating for the voiceless whenever possible.

As mentioned in this book Jill is also an Endometriosis warrior who is bringing awareness to those she can reach while encouraging a network of support.

CONNECT WITH
Jill Petrowsky
ON SOCIAL MEDIA

Instagram: @j.petrowsky
Facebook: J.Petrowsky
Twitter: J.Petrowsky

@j_petrowsky

Website: www.penofjpetrowsky.com

CPSIA information can be obtained
at www.ICGtesting.com
Printed in the USA
BVHW010850151118
533021BV00012BA/99/P